Papa, find me again!

A Parable
By Nigel Morris

Papa Find Me Again!
ISBN: 9780977202331
Copyright © Nigel Morris 2013

For further information and permissions, please contact:
Nigel Morris | Nigel.Brian.Morris@gmail.com

To order, please contact:
The Book Cellar
5340 E. La Palma Ave
Anaheim, CA 92807
714 777 5400 | bookstore@vcfanaheim.com

Cover photograph, Frog in a Kettle,
printed by kind permission of Claudette Bejtovic

For

Augustyna Moon CaroleLynne Hartman

with love.

Thanks

Thank you is such an inadequate expression of my gratitude to the many people without whom this project could never have happened.

My love and respect to Greg and Katie Scherer, Joe Gorra, Deb Lockwood, Lance Pittluck, Sarah Hartman, Jim Fredericks, "my" gifted photographers: Claudette Bejtovic, John Doukas, Craig Lockwood, and Thel and Nyla Rountree. Last, but not least, to my amazing wife, Lynne, thank you for everything!

Prayer

For this reason I bow my knees before the Father, from whom the whole family in heaven and on earth derives its name, that He would grant you, according to the riches of His glory, to be strengthened with power through His Spirit in the inner man, so that Christ may dwell in your hearts through faith; and that you, being rooted and grounded in love, may be able to comprehend with all the saints what is the breadth and length and height and depth, and to know the love of Christ which surpasses knowledge, that you may be filled up to all the fullness of God.

Ephesians 3:14-19 NASB

Endorsements

"A beautiful parable that speaks to the real and broken parts of us in poignant ways. Pastor Nigel shares artistically how God used "a little child" to teach him about his Heavenly Papa's constant and abiding love."
- Dianne Buhler
Wife of the late Dr. Rich Buhler - Author, Radio Broadcaster, Speaker, Pastor

"Nigel has brought us a simply beautiful parable of God's "Papa" love. It is all at once insightful, disarming, moving, and playful. "Papa, Find Me Again!" is a wonderful reminder of God's extravagant love for us. Pick up a copy today!!"
- Casey Corum
Pastor, Worship Leader, Songwriter, Producer

"Looking for love in all the wrong places is more than a great hook to a famous country song. It is the story of humanity—from Adam and Eve to the latest OMG! or TMZ story. With beautiful imagery and engaging writing, in Papa Find Me Again, Nigel Morris helps us see that we don't have to live buried by the tyranny of our disordered desires, that Papa can find us, and that in being found we, in the words of Jesus, "never hunger and thirst again"."
- Todd Hunter
Anglican Bishop, Author of *"Our Favorite Sin"* (Former National Director, Vineyard USA)

"It is well known that Jesus was the first to address God as "Abba" which today would mean "Papa" or "Daddy". It was meant by Jesus to convey God's desire for us to have a tender, intimate, dependent love for Him. Pastor and Chaplain Nigel Morris knows how hard it is to relate to God in this way. Yet with skill and brutal honesty, Morris shares in this book how he grappled with obstacles and found a renewed relationship with God as Papa. One cannot read this book without receiving help in his own journey."
- J P Moreland
Distinguished Professor of Philosophy, Talbot School of Theology and Author

"Being found by the love you were always looking for. A profound thought beautifully captured in prose and image in this heartwarming book by Nigel Morris. My heart was moved. I believe yours will be also."
- Ed Piorek
Pastor and Author of *"The Father Loves You"*

"To know, to experience the love of the Father…. to have that love revealed and made real in such deep and yet normal events of life. Nigel Morris has shared a very personal and profound experience with us all. Read slowly, ponder and let this be your very own source of fresh water."
- Phil Strout
National Director, Vineyard USA and Author

Forward

Papa Find Me Again is a beautiful book written by a beautiful man!

I have known Nigel Morris now for 16 years and he is one of the most compassionate men I know. So where does this heart come from?

The Bible says we love because He first loved us. When we make real contact with the true and living God, He *rubs off* on us. We start to reflect His heart and His mind. This is one man's story of how God revealed His amazing love to him.

Our stories may not be exactly the same as Nigel's, but the same God is always seeking to communicate the height and depth and width and breadth of His love to every one of us. One of the Spirit's main roles in our lives is to *convince* us of how much our Abba, our Daddy God really, honestly and sincerely loves us. Depending on your back-story this may happen suddenly or take many years to really sink in.

I hope you enjoy my friend's words and images and experience the reality of your Papa's love.

Lance Pittluck
Senior Pastor of the Vineyard Church of Anaheim and
Elder in the Vineyard at Large.

Papa, find me again!

It has been a long time coming, but I'm sure glad it's here.

Just like the long awaited appearance of a once a week train that has finally decided to show up at some back of beyond, outside nowhere, scratch in the dirt excuse for a real railroad station, my time of waiting is over, and this *thing* that has eluded me for so long has pulled into my life ⊡ big time.

The *thing* I'm referring to is the ongoing process of receiving God's love. By that I mean, getting hold of the fact that God likes me, loves me completely, and is passionately involved in every aspect of my life!

Like so many, I've run from His love, avoided it, faked it, and generally looked and lusted for it in all the wrong places over the course of my life.

Then suddenly, without any prior notice or a *by your leave*, it finds me; powerfully transforming the arid, inhospitable places of my heart as effectively as the dramatic appearance of a huge locomotive alters a weary desert landscape.

It has been a long time coming, but I'm sure glad it's here.

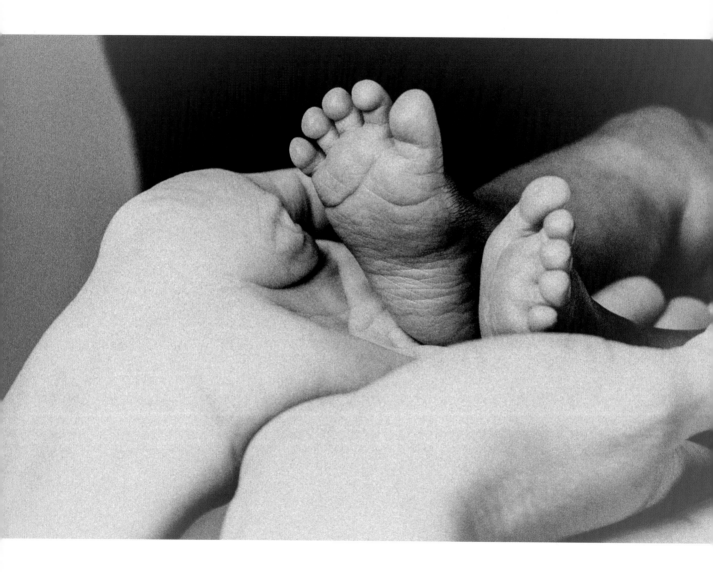

Nothing, however, could have prepared me for the manner in which it materialized.

To be accurate and honest (often hard to do in the same sentence) my granddaughter, is not my granddaughter through bloodline. She is the daughter of my stepdaughter and the closest I've ever come to having a child of my own.

Consequently, when she was born, all kinds of fatherly instincts and emotions washed over me and kicked me into a gear I never knew I had. She is two and a half as I am writing this.

No one informed me it was possible to fall so completely and utterly in love with someone I didn't know. I had no idea!

But there it was and there she was! Augustyna Moon CaroleLynne Hartman. Yep, all 31 letters of her! Fully capable of melting my heart and disarming me with her smile, at close or long range, anytime I looked at her.

Then when she started to call me *Papa*, the invasion was complete. My fate and future as a prisoner of her love was sealed as I willingly and joyfully surrendered to this tiny human being.

Gradually it dawned on me that although she was not strictly and theoretically my blood grandchild, practically and supremely importantly, I was her Papa and she was my Boo! And that, as they say, was the way things were going to be from then on.

I had much to learn from this new relationship.

One of her very favorite things to do is to play what she calls, *seek and hide*. It begins when she informs me with great authority, "I'm going to hide over there." She then proceeds to run just a short distance away and stand in plain sight.

Her hiding is complete when she puts both her hands over her eyes, thereby, convincing herself that I cannot possibly see her! The ritual continues. I count to ten and pretend to look for her, knowing, of course, where she is the whole time.

After a while, she'll giggle loudly and decide it's time to help me out by pretending to be some kind of small creature (her current favorite is the ribbit, ribbit of a frog). Finally, comes the grand moment and the great climax of my furtive seeking. I find her and declare triumphantly, "Boo, I've found you." She giggles as she throws her head back, delighted by this apparent sudden turn of events.

Then before I can catch my breath (finding someone who isn't lost is an exhausting business, after all) she'll say to me, "*Papa*, find me again." And we're off with more seeking and hiding.

A short while ago, as we were doing this for the fourth or maybe fifth time she said, as she usually does, *"Papa*, find me again." This time, that familiar phrase stopped me in my tracks; tears filled my eyes and my heart beat a little faster. Out of the blue, school was in session, and this was lesson time; only it was me who was the pupil and Augustyna Moon CaroleLynne Hartman, aged two and a half, was my God-given instructor.

The lesson went something like this: All my life I've searched for the elusive grail of the Father's unconditional love telling myself that perhaps this time it will come through this individual, through this means, or that circumstance. But of course, it never did, never does, or never can.

Until unexpectedly, through the voice of the small person standing in front of me, my eyes are opened to the way I have, effectively, played both roles in my version of this game, all too well, both the seeking and the hiding!

I've done more than my share of the seeking part; looking for the right thing but never in the right place! I was totally unaware that what I was desperately searching for was there all the time, hidden in plain sight, just like Augustyna.

While I was occupied in all that futile searching, I inadvertently became fully adept at doing the hiding part as well. Except, I've done more than innocently covering my eyes with my hands.

Over the course of my life I've hidden behind lies, guilt, and shameful behavior, hurting others and being hurt along the way, fearful to be really found and terrified to be truly known.

All the while He, my heavenly Father, has seen me. In fact, He has *never taken His eyes off me for a nanosecond.*

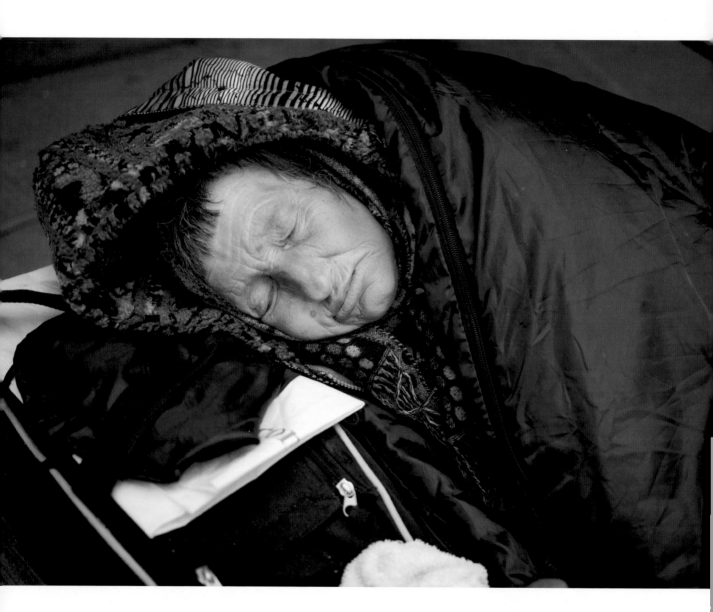

On the rare occasions I dared to glance in His direction, He appeared to be preoccupied elsewhere, so I gave up on Him, wrongly concluding that He couldn't possibly be interested in little ol' me.

I then reverted back to the old familiar routine of doing what I knew to do best, namely covering up and hiding.

And it is often when we're doing our *best* covering and our *best* hiding that He does His best finding! *Papas* are great at that, especially our heavenly one!

I remember that it was when I was at my worst, covered with guilt and shame, that my *Papa* found me in the first place. On this occasion the grand finale to my current lesson came when as someone once put it, *"He discovered himself again to me,"* through the voice of a little girl.

I like to think that as He did so, this time He was laughing and beaming with the sheer joy of the proudest, most loving *Papa* there ever was!

This is what I have learned thus far from my young tutor, Augustyna Moon.

I have learned afresh, that I can confidently say to my Heavenly Father anytime and anywhere...

"Papa, find me again, find me again. Find me again in this place, in this circumstance, in this confusion, in this difficulty, in this compulsive behavior, in this place of pain."

And do you know what? He always does and I believe He always will, because this *Papa* never ever gets tired of the seeking. He is *always*, hilariously and delightfully more overjoyed at the finding than it is possible for us to imagine, at least this side of heaven.

So, *Papa*, find me again.
Find me today, find me now!
Don't ever lose sight of where I am.
Don't ever let me wander
so far away from your Father's heart
of love and your strong life-giving embrace,
that I can't return to you in a moment...

to remain....perfectly and forever, found!

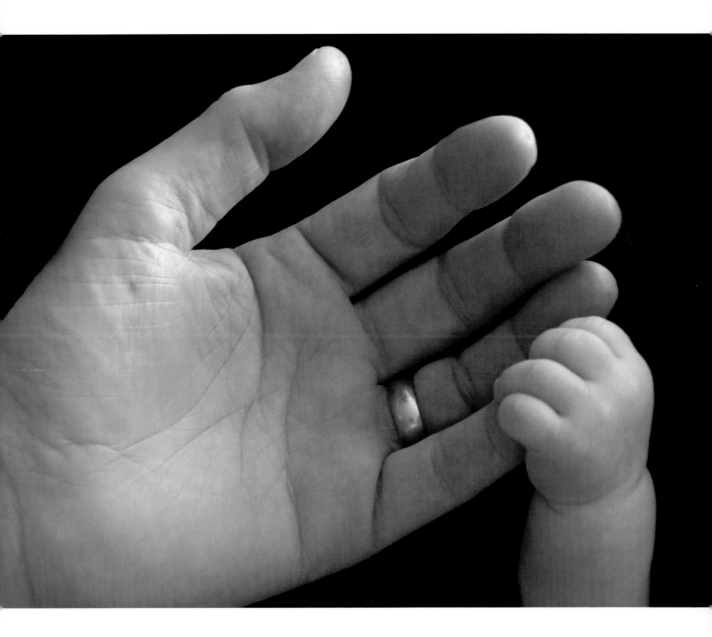

Prayer

Now to Him who is able to do exceeding, abundantly beyond all that we ask or think, according to the power that works within us, to Him be the glory in the church and in Christ Jesus to all generations forever and ever. Amen.

Ephesians 3:20-21 NASB

For Reflection

Within the parable, we are reminded of how we are designed to receive God's no-strings-attached kind of love. What kinds of desires, needs, and longings are stirred for you when you read this parable?

Nigel states that receiving God's love involves, "Getting hold of the fact that God likes me, loves me completely, and is passionately involved in every aspect of my life!" How does that sit with you? Do you believe that? Is that a fact that marks your experience with God? Ponder that, and consider what it might mean for you to grow, in a greater confidence, to receive God's love for every aspect of your life.

It might be tempting to think that receiving God's love is just another religious thing to do; that is, maybe you expect His love to only address the supposedly 'religious' or 'churchy' parts of your life. If so, how might the view of God presented by Nigel's challenge alter some of your views about God's love and His desire to transform the totality of your life?

It's easy to be preoccupied with thinking that we receive God's love only through particular means, the same way all the time. The result: "looking for the right thing in everywhere but the right place!" as Nigel says. It's tempting to 'pigeon-hole' the work of God. Can you identify some ways where your own imagination needs to be broadened and enlightened regarding what God is like and how he works? Regular acquaintance with His revelation of Himself through scripture is fruitful here.

Have you ever found yourself fearful to really be found and terrified to be truly known? What has that covering-up and hiding been like for you, whether in whole or in part? How has it affected your openness to receiving God's love?

When you consider your everyday routines in any given week (e.g., being a parent, going to work or school, etc), what are some areas of your life that need to be open to receiving, anew, God's love? Consider regularly praying throughout the day, "Papa, find me again in this [particular area/situation] of my life." At the end of your day, consider with gratitude the ways that God has seemed to be present to you. Consider how you might live/work differently in light of His loving, life-giving embrace upholding you.